D0952986

Mumbet: The Life and Times of Elizabeth Freeman

Portrait courtesy of Massachusetts Historical Society

Mumbet: The Life and Times of Elizabeth Freeman

The True Story of a Slave Who Won Her Freedom

Mary Wilds

Avisson Press, Inc.

Greensboro

 For information, contact Avisson Press Inc., P.O. Box 38816, Greensboro, North Carolina 27438 USA.

First edition
Printed in the United States of America
ISBN 1-888105-40-2

Library of Congress Cataloging-in-Publication Data

Wilds, Mary, 1960-

Mumbet : the life and times of Elizabeth Freeman : the true story of a slave who won her freedom / Mary Wilds. — 1st ed.

p. cm. — (Avisson young adult series)

Includes bibliographical references and index.

Summary: A biography of the eighteenth-century female slave whose court case helped to set precedents that would bar slavery in Massachusetts.

ISBN 1-888105-40-2 (lib. bdg.)

1. Freeman, Elizabeth, 1744?-1829 Juvenile literature. 2. Women slaves—Massachusetts Biography Juvenile literature. 3. Slaves-Massachusetts Biography Juvenile literature. 4. Afro-American women—Massachusetts Biography Juvenile literature. 5. Massachusetts Biograph Juvenile literature. 6. Slavery--Massachusetts—History—18th century Juvenile literature. [1. Freeman, Elizabeth, 1744?-1829. 2. Slaves. 3. Afro-Americans Biography. 4. Women Biography.] I. Title. II. Series.

E444.W566 1999

974.4'03'092—dc21

[B] 99-20017

CIP

Contents

Foreword

Eighty years before the Emancipation Proclamation was signed during the American Civil War, an enslaved Massachusetts woman named Elizabeth Freeman —better known to her masters and her community as Bett, or Mumbet — filed a landmark lawsuit at the Berkshire County Court of Common Pleas in Great Barrington, Massachusetts. In the lawsuit she demanded that her master, John Ashley of Sheffield, set her free. Her representative in court was a young Sheffield attorney, Theodore Sedgwick, who would one day serve in the United States Congress and on the Massachusetts Supreme Court.

It was not unusual for a Massachusetts slave to

go to court. Slaves in that colony had the right to sue for property in civil court. Many Massachusetts blacks had already used the courts to gain their freedom. But before the Elizabeth Freeman case, such lawsuits always hinged on a broken promise. A slave would swear before the court that his master had promised to free him when he met certain conditions. For example, a master would agree to free the slave when he reached the age of 21, then renege on the promise. But in the case of Elizabeth Freeman, no such promise had been made. Theodore Sedgwick's daughter, Catharine, wrote a short biography of Bett many years later. In it, she described the event that prompted Bett to file her lawsuit. In the spring of 1781, Bett had heard the Declaration of Independence read at a town meeting. She decided that its precepts of freedom and equality applied to her.

Therefore, when Theodore Sedgwick and his mentor, Connecticut attorney Tapping Reeve, took the case to court, they argued that Bett was not the lawful slave of their neighbor, John Ashley, *because slavery itself was unlawful.* According to one of Sedgwick's biographers, he also argued that slavery was incompatible with the statements of liberty put forth in the Massachusetts State Constitution, which had been passed only one year earlier, in 1780.

The Elizabeth Freeman case is not the one given credit for abolishing slavery in Massachusetts. The Quok Walker case, also tried in 1781, gets that honor. The Freeman lawsuit is, however, a famous and honored case in New England. It is also important for its use of the same ideology which helped the colonists win their freedom from England.

Elizabeth Freeman won her lawsuit and lived the rest of her life as a free woman. Since she left no words of her own about her life or the lawsuit that made her famous, there is no way of knowing how she felt about her experience, her contribution or her place in history. But we do know how she felt about freedom. In Bett's biography, Catharine Sedgwick writes the following:

> I have heard her say with an emphatic shake of the head peculiar to her, "Any time, any time while I was a slave, if one minute's freedom had been offered to me and I had been told I must die at the end of

> that minute, I would have taken it, just to stand one minute on God's earth a free woman, I would.'"[1]

This is the story of that remarkable woman, and of her life and times, a slave who by her own efforts became free.

Chapter 1

History knows Elizabeth Freeman by many names. She is referred to, in various historical accounts, as Betty, Bett, Mum Bett, or Mumbet. We don't know if her proper name was Elizabeth, or if it was a name she adopted upon gaining her freedom. We also don't know when or why she took the name Freeman, although male slaves who won their freedom by fighting in the Revolutionary War were known to take (or be given) the name "Freeman." She may have been following their lead.

As noted earlier, Elizabeth left no letters of her own, no diaries, no first-hand clues to her thinking or her way of seeing the world. The one document she did leave behind was a will: in it, she identifies herself as Elizabeth Freeman and lists her bequests, mentioning a daughter, also named Elizabeth, a granddaughter, Marianne Dean, three great-granddaughters and a great-grandson.[2] There is also her portrait, now kept at the Massachusetts Historical Society and painted by Susan Sedgwick, the daughter-in-law of the man who represented Freeman in court. Painted when Freeman was probably in her 60s, the portrait depicts a woman whose soft, round features belie the steely look in her eyes.

Most of what we know of Elizabeth Freeman comes from the letters, diaries, personal papers, and memoirs of those who apparently knew —and loved — her best.

Freeman was an immensely popular woman during her lifetime and today remains a famous historical figure in Berkshire County, Massachusetts. So much folklore has grown up around her and her freedom lawsuit that some historians have a hard time separating fact from fiction. Some also dispute whether it was her lawsuit or the one brought by a Barre slave, Quok Walker (or both), which brought about the end of slavery in Massachusetts. No one would dispute, however, that Freeman sued for her freedom in at a time when women could not vote, serve on juries or participate formally in the political process.

We know beyond a doubt that Elizabeth Freeman was owned by one of Sheffield, Massachusetts' most prominent and well-liked citizens. Col. John Ashley Jr. was the son of one of the town's founders — he was what we today would undoubtedly call a "mover and shaker." His father, also named John, had joined a band of pioneers who set out in 1722 to tame what was then the Massachusetts Bay Colony's western frontier. Armed with orders from the General Court of Massachusetts to organize settlements along the Housatonic River, they purchased land from the Indians, cut a narrow road through the mountains and carved a village in the middle of the wilderness. [3]

Col. John Ashley Jr. was a Yale graduate, a lawyer, mill owner, moderator at town meetings, selectman, justice of the peace, merchant judge and representative to the Massachusetts General Court. He was an officer of distinction who led the First Foot Company of Sheffield. [4]

While on a business trip to Claverack Landing, New York, (where he used to drive his father's cattle for trade), he met a Dutch girl named Annetje (or Hannah) Hockaboom (or Hogeboom), youngest daughter of the well-to-do Pieter (or Peter) Hogeboom.[5] The Ashleys are said to have wed in 1735, shortly before John Ashley built the now-famous Ashley House. Today, Ashley House is a popular tourist attraction in South Sheffield, three-quarters of a mile west of Ashley Falls, a nearby hamlet named for the Ashley family. (The house, originally built on the banks of the Housatonic River, was moved to its present location in 1930.) [6]

John Ashley spared no expense to make his home — which boasted deep fireplaces, small-paned windows and a curved staircase — into a showplace. It was there that he and Hannah raised their four children, and there that a young slave known as Bett came to live. (When Ashley died in 1802, at the age of 92, he left some 3,000 acres, 17 houses, eight barns, a grist mill, a cider mill and his ironworks to his three surviving children.)[7]

There are several stories of when and how Bett came to live with the Ashleys. A local

Berkshires history book, "The Chronicles of Old Canaan," makes mention that Hannah's father, Peter Hogeboom, bequeathed "all of his Negroes and negresses" to his children upon his death in 1746. Bett was said to have been about 14 at that time, and to have gone to the Ashleys shortly after Hogeboom's death.[8]

Another story, attributed to the Ashley family, says that Bett had come to Ashley House as an infant two years earlier, in 1744.[9] This story, as depicted in a 1973 account of Bett's life, goes on to paint a charming picture of little Bett, barely six months old and bundled-up against the cold, lying in the bottom of a straw-filled sleigh, on her way to a new home in the middle of winter.[10]

But at least one source, an article written by Mimi MacDonald in the *Berkshire Courier*, dated July 6, 1981, casts some doubt on this account. Macdonald points out that Bett is said to have had a younger sister, Lizzie, who came with her to Ashley House. If this is true, a six-month-old child was unlikely to have had a younger sibling.[11]

Although Lizzie could have been an older sister, her place in all the stories suggests otherwise. Bett is always portrayed as Lizzie's protector, watching over her "as a lioness might watch over her cubs"[12]— which hardly sounds like a role a younger sibling would take.

MacDonald goes on to speculate that the "Lizzie" mentioned in all the accounts of Bett's life might have actually been Bett's daughter, Elizabeth.[13] This could either mean that Bett was a very young woman or a teenager when she came to live with the Ashleys — and the baby at the bottom of the sleigh might have been her own daughter — or (in a more likely scenario) she was an infant who came alone to the Ashleys, grew up with them and bore her child many years later while living at Ashley House.

Since Bett had no birth certificate and since no records of her sale or any other transactions involving her survive, her exact age upon arriving at the Ashleys must remain conjecture. However, when Bett died in 1829, the Sedgwick family, who remained among her closest friends (and who are said to have dubbed her with the nickname, "Mum Bett"), guessed that Bett died "in her 85th year." If the Sedgwicks were correct about her age, this would mean that she was 37 when she filed her freedom lawsuit in 1781 — and that she had indeed been born in 1744, the year she is said to have come to Ashley House.

Yet, among the long list of bequests to daughter Elizabeth in Freeman's will is the mention of a "short gown that was my mother's."[14] One would have to wonder if even the kindest, most caring master would remember to send a family keepsake along with a slave baby on her way to a new home.

Chapter 2

Whenever or however Elizabeth Freeman came to the Ashleys, at one point she was married and did have a child. The name of her husband has been lost to history; we know nothing about him except that he fought, and died, in the Revolutionary War. We don't even know if his name, too, was Freeman; if he took it upon entering the military, and if Elizabeth took the name before or after his death.

Henry Dwight Sedgwick, the son of the attorney who represented Freeman in her lawsuit, noted in a speech at the Lyceum in Stockbridge in February, 1831, that "she was married when young; her husband died soon after, in the continental service in Revolutionary War, leaving her with one child."[15] A biographer of the

Sedgwick family later recorded that in Massachusetts military records there were several soldiers listed as "Freeman", including Abner, Ely, Jonathan and Phillip of Sheffield, and Caesar of Great Barrington.[16] There is no record of marriage or any other kind of link between them and Elizabeth Freeman.

Such lack of documentation in the life of a colonial slave is not unusual. Negro slaves were considered as chattel or property and were taxed as such. This attitude was deeply entrenched in the northern colonies, ever since the first slaves had been brought to Boston in 1638.[17] Slaves like Elizabeth were allowed to marry, but masters were also allowed to sell their spouses or children, who could be packed up at a moment's notice and sent elsewhere. Such actions were deemed perfectly acceptable. An article in a 1746 edition of the *Boston Evening Post* termed it "very surprizing (sic)" that a local Negro couple should be so devoted to one another as to commit suicide upon learning that the woman would soon be sold "into the country."

It may seem odd to modern sensibilities that, in the midst of their drive for freedom from English rule, American colonists were blind to the fact that an enslaved people lived among them. But at the time of the Revolutionary War, many white colonists in the North and South sincerely believed that Africans were ordained by God to serve the white race. Slave trading was considered both an honorable and lucrative profession. Three of Massachusetts' most respected judges, John Saffin, John Coleman and John Campbell, were slave merchants. Two Massachusetts slave traders, William Pepperell and Charles Hobby, became so well-liked and prominent that the English Crown knighted them.[18]

The nature and quality of slave life probably depended upon whom one asked. Catharine Sedgwick, a white woman who grew up in a comfortable household, began her biographical essay on Bett with this description of slavery:

> "Before the American Revolution slavery extended throughout the United States, In New England (slavery) was on a very limited scale," she wrote. "There were household slaves in Boston who drove the coaches and cooked the dinners and shared the luxuries of rich houses, and a few were distributed among the most wealthy of the rural

> population. They were not numerous enough to make the condition a great evil or embarrassment, but quite enough to show its incompatibility with the demonstration of the truth that all men are born equal and have a inalienable right to life. No doubt there were hard masters and cruel mistresses and so there are cruel fathers and exacting mothers — unrestrained power is not a fit human trust."[19]

Her brother Henry, during his lecture on the Freeman case given 50 years after his father helped to free Bett, had a similar opinion of slavery.

"Slavery in New York and New England was so masked that but a slight difference could be perceived in the condition of slaves and hired servants," he said. "The younger slaves not only ate and drank, but played with the children. They thus became familiar companions to each other. The black women were cooks and nurses, and such assisted by their mistresses ... In this state of familiar intercourse instances of cruelty were uncommon, and ... caused a degree of indignation not much less if committed on a freeman."[20]

Catharine was right to say that slaves weren't plentiful in New England. The black population of Massachusetts peaked at 5,298 in 1765. Blacks were actually never more than 2.2 percent of that colony's population.[21] However, slave traffic *was* a linchpin of the northern economy. New England was the home of the Triangular Trade, which linked New England, Africa and West Indian plantations.

The Triangular Trade worked like this: sugar, molasses and rum from the West Indies were exchanged for farm produce, lumber and manufactured goods made in New England. New Englanders used the West Indian sugar and molasses to make rum. Africa, in return for the rum New England made, supplied West Indian sugar plantations with slaves.[22]

In Massachusetts, the slave trade boomed. Thousands of sailors, tanners, coopers and sailmakers serviced the slave fleets. The slave trade built such huge profits that a number of related industries — distilling, agriculture, ship building —mushroomed around it. Slaves could be found everywhere in Massachusetts, but were most common in the commercial and industrial counties of Suffolk, Essex and Plymouth, where the jobs were plentiful and where most white colonists also lived.[23] The colonies, remarked New York Governor Samuel Bellmont during a visit to the New York Board of Trade, "have no other servants but Negroes available to do the work." [24]

Slaves may have been domestic servants but they were also bakers, tailors, sailmakers, weavers, coopers, blacksmiths, goldsmiths, cabinetmakers, naval carpenters, shoemakers, brushmakers and glaziers.[25] Boston engraver Thomas Fleet employed a talented slave in his printing shop. The slave set type, cut wooden blocks for engraving, and put out most of the illustrations Fleet was known for.[26] A Massachusetts man named Peter Cross owned a slave known throughout the region as an excellent sailor. This slave was so much in demand that eventually Cross allowed him to take charge of a ship. The many whaling boats that set out from New Bedford, Massachusetts, used slave crew members; sometimes, observers said, half the crew was black.[27]

Because skilled labor of any kind was scarce in the colonies, masters often hired out their slaves to fellow craftsmen or farmers. (Women were hired out as laundresses or housekeepers.) He who hired the slave would pay him or her a salary, and give them meals and a place to stay. The master received a portion of the slave's wages, and the slave kept what was left. The very best of the slave craftsmen knew how to bargain for better wages and better food and clothing. More importantly, they were able to save enough money to buy their freedom and that of their families. [28]

Slaves in the Northern Colonies had limited protection under the law. They were encouraged to set a "government" within their communities for settling slave disputes. They'd be asked to elect a "governor," and sheriffs and judges. The election process got to be so popular that a master's social standing might rise or fall depending on how well his slave fared as a candidate. In some villages, slaves even got a three-day holiday to celebrate. On the other hand, all candidates had to be approved by the masters prior to the election; so-called "rebellious" slaves were not allowed to run. Masters must have figured it was a way to bring slave leaders into the white power structure and reduce the risk of a slave rebellion at the same time. [29]

Life on the frontier wasn't all work and struggle. White settlers tried hard to turn work projects into social events. A barn-raising might turn into a community party. If a woman needed to spend a day or so weaving cloth, she'd invite a neighbor to help her. The two women would sit side-by-side, working, gossiping and trading news and ideas.[30]

Blacks of that day knew how to have fun, too, but they had to carve it out of their work schedule. They did their socializing together, and away from most whites. Little is known of slave life in the 18th century because much of it was kept secret. We do know, however, that groups of slaves would meet whenever they could in hospitable taverns, private homes, or in warehouses on the back streets. Historian Richard C. Wade called this part of slave culture "alley society."[31]

It seems that all the curfews in the world could not stop "alley society." A Boston newspaper article of 1738 described a "parcel of negroes" who met for a party, bringing with them bread, sugar, "fowls" and rum. (Unfortunately for the merrymakers, they'd chosen a dwelling that caught fire during the night. They were forced to throw their food into the harbor, and flee.) [32]

Another Massachusetts newspaper account dated two years later told of a white Bostonian who walked into a Roxbury tavern and found "about a dozen black gentry, he's and she's, in a very merry humour, singing and dancing, having a violin and store of wine and punch before them."[33]

Slave funerals became social occasions because a death was one of the few times blacks could gather together unbothered by the white establishment. Black funerals often made the newspapers in the 18 century. Newspaper articles of that time describe black funerals that were adorned with every bell and whistle. Even sympathetic white town officials came to pay their respects. The more prominent the black person, the more elaborate the funeral.[34]

Recognizing social prominence during a burial seems to have had its roots in African traditions. According to anthropologist Melville J. Herskovits, in West Africa the deceased "must have a funeral in keeping with his position in the community if he is to take his rightful place in the afterlife." Thus, blacks in New England who were well-thought of always got put to rest with dancing, singing and feasting.[35]

As for every-day life for a New England slave, McManus observes in his book, *Black Bondage in the North*, that most slaves did receive adequate food, shelter, clothing and medical care — they were, after all, an investment in their masters' eyes. Slave housing depended on how wealthy their master was, or the size of his home. In the city, slaves usually lived in cellars or garrets. In rural areas they would live in outbuildings next to the main house.[36]

Masters also gave their slaves clothing appropriate for the harsh New England weather. Some even provided their slaves with "Sunday clothes" in addition to a working wardrobe for every day.[37]

The slave living in 18th century America probably had strong ties to Africa. Even if the slave wasn't born there, his parents may have been, or a relative, or his friends. Slaves openly cherished their African heritage. A man visiting Boston in 1638 described his encounter with a singular and regal slave woman. She insisted she'd been a queen in her homeland and refused to mate with the man her master had chosen for her

— such a man was apparently beneath her.[38]

A free black man named Pompey was regarded by all who knew him as an African king. Pompey was treated accordingly throughout his life. Once a year slaves from Boston, Salem and elsewhere would visit him at his home in Lynn. The gathering invariably turned into a festival. Visiting children placed wild flowers on Pompey's head while he and other elders recounted stories from their African youth.[39]

A Deerfield, Massachusetts woman by the name of Jin was known to have saved bits of cloth, glass, crockery, stones, and buttons — anything she fancied. Like other blacks, she believed her spirit would go home to Africa after she died and she wanted to have things to bring with her home.[40]

Some slaves didn't wait for the afterlife. They simply packed up and went back to Africa as soon as they got the money and the opportunity. The *Boston Evening Post* related the story of a Rhode Island couple who "by their industry and frugality ... scraped together two or three hundred pounds ... sail'd from Newport for New Guinea."[41]

Activists who petitioned the Massachusetts legislature for their freedom often referred to themselves as Africans. One eloquent black letter-writer described slaves as a free people upon whom America had temporarily placed its heavy yoke. A slave poet, Deliverance, who lived in Danvers, Massachusetts, put this statement into her verse: "they stole us from Africa, the home of the free, And brought us in bondage across the blue sea." [42]

Chapter 3

Slaves in Massachusetts were luckier than their counterparts elsewhere in the world. They couldn't serve on juries but did have the right to a jury trial. They had the right to own some personal property, like clothing. If the slave's master wanted the slave's property, the law stipulated he should buy it.[43] If he refused, the slave could sue him in court and demand its return.

It was a crime to deliberately kill or injure a slave. However, such a crime was difficult to prove — especially if it was the master who did it. Slaves were beaten if they violated curfew and could carry nothing, not even a walking stick, that even remotely resembled a weapon.[44]

Slaves tried any number of ways to win their

freedom. As noted earlier, some were able to buy it. Others tried escaping. Despite help from such unlikely sources as the Seneca and Onondaga Indian tribes of northern New York (who were known to welcome escaped slaves into their tribes), most fugitives were eventually captured.[45]

In 1626, eleven slaves owned by the West India Company of New Netherlands (later New York) asked for their freedom. They had spent long years, they said, building roads and settlements for white settlers and deserved a reward for it all. The company did free them, but on one condition: they had to pay their former owners a fee once a year: "30 skepels of maize or wheat, peas or beans, and one fat hog." If they refused to pay it, their freedom would be revoked, the company said. The group was also given a parcel of swampy land upon which to build their own settlement. (That "swampy land" is now the Greenwich Village section of New York City.)

Of course, negotiation rarely worked, much to the frustration of those who tried it. Between Jan. 6, 1773, and Feb. 10, 1780, blacks asked Massachusetts officials to abolish slavery no less than eight times. Several of the petitions were written by a prominent free black man known as Prince Hall, a resident of Boston. Hall went on to found the first Black Masonic Order in America, the Boston African Lodge and the first black school in Boston. [46]

The appeals from Hall and the others were almost entirely ignored. Not even compromises and halfway measures got the legislators' attention. A group of men who wrote a letter dated April 20, 1773 urged the colonists to adopt a Spanish tradition that would at least give American slaves hope. Spaniards, the men said, allowed their slaves one free day a week to earn money towards their purchase price. Other petitioners asked that their children be set free at the age of 21.[47]

Those who petitioned the courts and the legislature espoused some of the same ideas white colonists used in their struggle with Mother England. After April 1773, as talk of a revolution grew more heated, slaves demanded their "natural rights." They argued that their situation among whites was far worse than England's treatment of the colonists.[48]

"Every principle from which America has acted in the course of her unhappy difficulties with Great Britain pleas stronger than a thousand arguments in favor of your petitioners," black petitioners wrote in 1777. [49]

The one strategy that did appear to work was the freedom lawsuit. Slaves were taking their masters to court as early as 1701. Since there were no class action suits in those days, slaves appeared in court on their own. They usually made their case by claiming that their masters had reneged on a promise to free them. This was apparently something almost no judge of that area would tolerate. In 1701, a slave named Adam charged that his master, John Saffin of Boston, had violated a contractual obligation to free him. He won the suit two years later.[50]

In 1735, a deceased Bostonian's son tried to claim that he had inherited a slave named James from his father. James contended that in his will his late master had freed him, and that the will had been misplaced. Despite threats against his life, James continued with the suit. The court freed him two years later. A woman named Jenny Slew of Ipswich, Mass., lost a suit for freedom in 1762, but won it on appeal three years later.[51]

Not surprisingly, freedom lawsuits increased as tensions between England and the colonies escalated with the fervent talk of liberty. But although the slave almost always won his case, not until the 1780s would slavery end in the Bay Colony. For obvious reasons, some blacks weren't willing to wait. A small number of them turned to violence. In 1735, two slaves were convicted of trying to kill their owners with poisoned chocolate. They were sentenced to sit for an hour on the gallows with a rope around their necks and then to be whipped, 39 lashes apiece.[52]

In 1751, a slave woman tried to poison her owner's children with ratsbane. She was executed. Four years later, two slaves by the name of Mark and Phillis were hung and burned at the stake, respectively, for the poisoning of Captain John Codman of Charlestown.[53]

One notorious case involved a Massachusetts slave woman known as Black Maria. Maria was convicted of setting fire to two houses in Roxbury. A small child died in that fire. Maria was convicted and burned at the stake. Newspapers of the day picked up on many stories of arson and murder allegedly perpetrated by slaves.[54]

Robert Twombly, in his article "Black Resistance to Slavery in Massachusetts," observes that, somehow, most white colonists never seemed to connect these violent acts with the obvious: that an entire people lived in slavery. Rather, the whites preferred to think that blacks had a weak character. They were untrustworthy, immoral, sinful and vicious, but not rebellious. [55]

The colonists enacted a long list of laws meant to curb such "character defects" in their slaves. In 1686, Massachusetts passed a statute that prohibited blacks and other servants from buying and drinking alcohol. Sixty years later, the Massachusetts House of Representatives passed a new law that forbade slaves and sailors to swear. In 1756 the Bay colony decreed that no one, "especially slaves," would be allowed to start a bonfire within 10 "rods" of a house.[56]

Blacks and whites were also not allowed to marry, a relatively new cultural development. Early on, there'd been a number of attachments between Northern blacks and whites of both sexes. It was not unheard of for a white woman to marry a black man or even her slave. The reason for such marriages was simple: in New England, white women outnumbered white men.[57]

The children of black-white unions were called mulattos. By the 1700s, New Englanders had become alarmed at what they saw as a growing, mixed-race population. Massachusetts passed strict laws against what was then called miscegenation. Black-white marriages were outlawed. Any black man "found guilty" of sexual relations with a white woman was flogged, or beaten, and sold away out of the colony, whether or not he had been a slave at the time of their liaison. The woman with whom he'd been involved was also flogged and forced to become an indentured servant so she could support any children from their union. If a white man had a liaison with a black woman, he was flogged, fined and forced to support whatever children the two had had together. The woman was also flogged and sold out of the colony. This law applied to both free blacks and slaves. Thus, those free blacks who dared a relationship with a white man or woman risked a return to bondage.[58]

Not surprisingly, New Englanders began to encourage marriage within its slave population. In 1705, Massachusetts forbade any master to "deny marriage to his Negro with one of the same nation, any law, usage or custom to the contrary notwithstanding." A slave owned by one master was allowed to marry the slave owned by another as long as both masters agreed to it.[59]

Even well-known Puritan clergymen like Cotton Mather, Ezra Stiles and Samuel Sewall officiated at slave marriages. However, these marriages must have carried a built-in poignancy. Marriage didn't guarantee that one spouse or the other, or their children, wouldn't be sold.[60]

New England's attitude towards its slaves did not begin to change for many years, yet, even in the early 1700s, there was a very vocal group of free blacks and whites who insisted that slavery was wrong.

One of the founders of this new movement — which came to be known as abolition — was a Southern Berkshires Congregationalist minister named Samuel Hopkins. Born in Waterbury, Connecticut, and educated at Yale, Hopkins came to Great Barrington in 1743. Though he probably developed the first drafts of his many sermons on the evils and inequities of Negro slavery while at his Berkshire parish, his tenure in Great Barrington was not a happy one. Religious and political differences forced him to ask the parish for his dismissal in 1769.[61]

Hopkins moved to a new parish in Newport, R.I., where, ironically enough, he became an ardent slavery opponent while preaching in one of the biggest slave-trading ports in the country. His major work, *Dialogue on Slavery*, won the support of John Jay and Alexander Hamilton and was issued by them to every member of Congress.[62]

Men like Hopkins, though, were few and far between. The slaves of 18th century New England had few white champions. Blacks were considered objects of fate, antisocial deviants, children to be protected or chastised, or commodities.[63] Even abolitionists put their scruples aside when necessary. Patriot leaders James Warren and John Adams opposed an abolition bill put before the Massachusetts House. They feared such a bill might alienate their southern colleagues and polarize the colonies.

Catharine Sedgwick, Theodore's daughter, came to love Elizabeth Freeman like a mother. Yet, in Freeman's biography, Catharine wrote, "The effect of a gentle nature is apparent in the subservient manner of the colored people whether in slavery or freedom. (Mum Bett) is a striking exception to this truth. She perfectly maintained the decorum of her station but she had not one particle of the subservency of caste. Her intelligence, her integrity, her resolute mind were apparent in her deportment and gave her an unquestioned ascendancy over her companions in service."[64]

Chapter 4

By all accounts, John Ashley was a man without enemies. He was apparently one of those rare souls who retained compassion for his fellow men while continuing to build a tremendous fortune. He was the man behind Sheffield's new, riverfront grist mill. He had interests in iron mines and quarries. He bought up a great deal of the fertile farmland in the Housatonic river valley. In the heavily wooded hills surrounding Sheffield, Ashley's men operated lumber mills and made charcoal. (His father, John Sr., obtained Sheffield's first sawmill charter in 1731. This same mill planed the wooden planks which would line Sheffield's Great Road, also begun in 1731.)[65]

The Ashley name is entwined with one of the southern Berkshire's more famous landmarks,

Bartholomew's Cobble. The "cobble" is a set of picturesque and rocky knolls in the southern half of what is now Sheffield, just above the Connecticut border. The Quartzite and marble sediment were laid in the cobble millions of years ago when Massachusetts was still covered by sea water. (The Ashley family owned the cobble for a time in the 1700s. The Cobble got its name, however, from a 19th century owner, George Bartholomew. Designated by the United States Department of the Interior as a National Natural Landmark, the Cobble is both a western Massachusetts tourist attraction and home to five-million-year old rocks, Indian artifacts, and 235 species of birds.) [66]

The teenage John Ashley Jr. helped his father survey the southern Berkshire frontier. Young Ashley had been born in Westfield, Mass., on Dec. 2, 1709. He was graduated from Yale University in 1730 and admitted to the Hampshire Bar two years later. And, almost continuously over the next 40 years, he was the man to know in Sheffield.

Lillian Preis, author of *Sheffield, Frontier Town*, quotes one Robert Taylor as saying, "Sheffield people did scarcely anything without

Ashley's having a hand in it."[67] On May 22, 1735, he was given a special job during the raising of Sheffield's meeting house. He was one of two men in charge of handing out the beverages supplied to the workers (a task that must have required a sober mind and steady heart); he also served as pinman to the crew. A book on the Ashley family, the *Ashley Genealogy*, records that "On Nov. 7 Ensign Ashley, Dr. Nathaniel Downing and Nathaniel Austin were chosen to lay the affairs of the town before the General Assembly at Boston."[68]

Ashley served on all the best town committees. He was chosen to settle differences between a Rev. Jonathan Hubbard, his church and the town. In the earliest years of that same church he was given "a right to build a pew," an honor only given to townsmen with high social ranking. In November 1761, his fellow Sheffield residents asked him to divvy out the seats in the meetinghouse.[69]

Hannah Hogeboom Ashley, John's wife, was — allegedly — as unlikable as her husband was likable. Catharine Sedgwick, daughter of Elizabeth Freeman's attorney and America's first popular woman novelist, wrote this vivid description of Col. and Mrs. John Ashley's marriage:

The plan of Providence to prevent monstrous discrepancies, by mating the tall with the short, the fat with the lean, the sour with the sweet ... was illustrated by ... [Colonel] Ashley and his help-meet. He was the gentlest, most benign of men and she was a shrew, untamable ....[70]

Hannah played quite a prominent role in Catharine Sedgwick's account of Bett's life. In another tale recorded by Sedgwick, a young and troubled neighbor girl comes to the Ashley House to ask for help.

When Madam got half across the kitchen, in full sight of the child, (Bett said) she turned to me, and her eyes flashing like a cat's in the dark, she asked me, "what that baggage wanted?"

"To speak to master," (Bett says.)

"What does she want to say to your master?"

"I don't know, ma'am."

"I know," she said — and there was no foul thing she didn't call the child.[71]

Obviously, Hannah Ashley is ready to turn the child out, but Bett commands the girl to "sit still, child."

"Madam (Ashley) knew when I set my foot down, I kept it down," Sedgwick records Bett as saying. And, so the story goes, the young girl got to see John Ashley.[72]

In another, more dramatic episode, Bett's sister (or daughter) Lizzie, hungry for extra food, had stolen the scraps left over from the Ashleys' meal. Hannah Ashley discovered her actions and went into a fury. She took a red-hot shovel used to clean away ashes from the fireplace and went after Lizzie with it.[73]

Bett, ever the big sister, stepped in front of Lizzie and took the blow for her. The red-hot shovel left a scar that Bett carried the rest of her life. It was a scar, Catharine Sedgwick said, that Bett was wont to wear like a badge. If anyone was to ask about it, Catharine said, Bett would only say, "Ask missus."[74]

Some historians cast a skeptical eye on such stories, dismissing them as folklore created in the same vein as George Washington and his cherry tree and Ben Franklin and his kite. Nonetheless, it would still be safe to say that John Ashley enjoyed a much better reputation than did his wife. For one thing, he was a patriot and a supporter of American Independence — albeit a cautious one.

Of course, the whole of the American colonies was filled with cautious patriots. Even in the wake of the first shots fired at Lexington, many considered the struggle to be over their rights as British citizens. No less than George Washington himself, when he took command of the Continental Army, said: "I abhor the idea of American Independence."[75]

The Massachusetts frontier certainly had its share of cautious patriots. Sheffield, along with most of its neighbors, deliberated and stalled when urged by Boston to join its citizens in standing up to the British. The town also stood behind its most influential citizen, John Ashley, when he drew harsh criticism over his role in the infamous "circular letter" case.

In February, 1768, the House of Representatives sent a letter to every colonial assembly. The letter asked citizens to unite and oppose the Townshend Acts. (One commentator calls this letter a moderately worded protest of "taxation without representation.") British ministers, however, did not consider the letter mild. They called it treasonable and rebellious. Britain demanded that the Massachusetts governor Bernard have it rescinded. The House of Representatives was not intimidated by Britain's threats. By a vote of 92 to 17, legislators refused to withdraw the letter.[76]

When the people learned via the newspapers how each representative voted on the issue, the "glorious 92" were widely praised and the "infamous 17" were scorned. One of those 17 was John Ashley of Sheffield. (It was a decision that must have come back to haunt him more than once.) Some Berkshire residents were furious over Ashley's vote. The residents of nearby Great Barrington (the future setting for Bett's trial) were angry enough to censure Ashley at a meeting. Nonetheless, their displeasure was not enough to boot Ashley out of office. He was re-elected, along with two others who'd cast a "yes" vote: Jonathan Bliss and Israel Williams.[77]

Fortunately for Ashley, Sheffield was a conservative town. On Sept. 22, 1768 Bostonians put out a call for fellow Bay colonists to oppose the landing of new British troops, who were there to defend Boston customs officials. One hundred and four Bay colony towns sent sympathetic delegates. Sheffield sent none. In fact, not one Berkshire delegate joined the protest.[78]

In 1772, Sheffield once again refused to join with Boston. Sheffield had received a letter from that town's Committee of Correspondence asking all towns in the province to unite and resist England's decision to pay the salaries of the Supreme Court judges from customs revenues. Sheffield said no.[79] Still, it was only be a matter of time before Sheffield residents, like everyone else, gave in to the liberty fever. In the huge, second-floor study of Ashley house, eleven Sheffield men, including John Ashley, got together during the winter of 1772-73 and wrote what is known as the Sheffield Declaration of Independence. It was adopted as law at a town meeting on Jan. 12, 1773.[80]

The declaration read in part, "Mankind in a State of Nature are equal, free and independent of each other." Though less well-known than North Carolina's Mecklenberg Declaration which came two years later, Sheffield's was considered by some observers to be the colonies' first formal declaration of independence from England. Suddenly, the little southwestern corner of the

Massachusetts Bay Colony was a thorn in Mother England's side. [81]

"A flame has sprung up at the extremity of the province," General Gage, the commander of the British forces in the American colony, said in a letter to King George. "The popular rage is very high in Berkshire and makes its way to the rest." [82]

In the summer of 1774, some eight months before Lexington and Concord's "shot heard round the world," a crowd of 1,500 citizens demonstrated against English tax policies. Encouraged by the declaration drawn up at Ashley House, the people seized the courthouse at Great Barrington and prevented a session of King George's court from taking place. [83]

Once Berkshire residents made up their minds to join the patriot cause they threw themselves into it wholeheartedly. Sixty delegates, chosen by inhabitants of various Berkshire towns, met at the Red Lion Inn in Stockbridge on July 6, 1774. Ashley and Theodore Sedgwick were among them, and were chosen chairman and clerk, respectively. The convention delegates immed-iately adopted the following resolution:

"*(We) advise the inhabitants of this county to the non-consumption of British manufacturers, under such limitations and exceptions, as to them shall appear proper.*"[84]

The group also opted to boycott any British goods bought after October 1st of that year.

The Berkshires quickly raised two regiments of minutemen. By the following year these regiments were drilling regularly on the local green. When news of the battle of Lexington arrived in the Berkshires via stagecoach, the region's minutemen marched to Roxbury. They served in the vicinity of Boston until the British evacuated the area the following March.[85]

On June 18, 1776, the residents of Sheffield held a town meeting and voted almost unanimously that the American Colonies should be free from Great Britain, and that Sheffield should throw its weight behind the Revolution.[86]

A liberty tree was erected in Sheffield, only to be cut down the following evening. An investigation immediately ferreted out the culprit: a local merchant, Dan Raymond. He was forced to walk between double lines of all the men and boys in town and ask each of them separately for forgiveness.[87]

During the Revolutionary War, Sheffield raised a total of $30,030 for its soldiers. Citizens also took care of the families those soldiers left at home. During a town meeting held on June 30, 1777, Sheffield residents decided that each non-commissioned officer and each private would receive two shillings per day while on the march and a shilling per day while in camp. On March 1778, the town voted to raise the money to buy a stock of powder, lead and flints and clothing for the army.[88]

Sheffield even had its own Revolutionary War hero. Ethan Allen, of the Green Mountain Boys, had settled his family on a farm in Sheffield in 1767. His three children, Lucy Caroline, Mary Ann and Joseph, were born in southern Berkshire, though Allen actually spent little time in the region or with his family. He, of course, went on to lead the Green Mountain Boys in the capture of Fort Ticonderoga and its much-coveted cannon.[89]

As the slave of John Ashley, local political leader and the most important man in town, Bett had a ringside seat for all the excitement. More importantly, she more than likely witnessed or overheard a number of political "bull" sessions between Ashley and his friends. One of Bett's more important duties in the Ashley household was to see to their guests. And at Ashley House, there were many guests. When Bett wasn't cooking, cleaning, washing clothes, dipping candles, making soap, baking bread, or taking care of Hannah Ashley's herb garden at the rear of the house, she was pouring beverages for John Ashley's guests or bringing them food.

Bett could neither read nor write, but surely the tenets of the new Massachusetts State Constitution — all men are created equal — must have been crystal clear to her. Besides, those were the days when the talk of freedom and a new country had to have been everywhere — in church, at local gathering places like corn-husking bees, house-raisings, quilting bees and harvest dinners, and of course, in Ashley House.

Momentous things had been happening since Sheffield declared its independence in 1774. The Continental Congress had signed the American Declaration of Independence and the Revolutionary War was being fought. Massachusetts sister colony, Vermont, had abolished slavery in 1777. The new state of Massachusetts had ratified its constitution in 1780, an event which Ashley and his friends surely must have celebrated.

Any intelligent person, man or woman, would have realized that dramatic changes were afoot. And it was one year after Massachusetts' new constitution became law that Bett, soon to be known as Elizabeth Freeman, decided to make a change of her own.

Chapter 5

One can safely assume that Bett's husband received his freedom upon going to war. Who knows what plans Bett and her husband might have had? Once he returned from the war, he might have worked to obtain their freedom from the Ashleys. He and his wife and daughter might have had their own home, and built their own life. Thus, Bett's hopes must have been high when her husband went off to war, only to see them dashed upon his death.

Slaves and freedmen like her husband played a significant role in the American Revolution. Probably the most famous of these was Crispus Attucks, the first man to die in the American Revolution. Attucks fought and died during the Boston Massacre. Thus, the first martyr to the

American cause was a black man. Later on, at Bunker Hill, a black soldier named Peter Salem would distinguish himself.

The Revolutionary War gave colonial slaves a bargaining chip. The British, realizing America's slaves were a potential fighting force, deliberately encouraged slave defections. The Crown offered freedom to runaway slaves who took refuge with England's army. Britain also made it clear that any black who supported the American cause would be treated harshly if caught. During a raid into northern New Jersey in 1779, British troops killed two Negro women for "endeavoring to drive off some cattle belonging to their masters."[90]

Enlistment opportunities on the American side increased as the war dragged on. The colonies found it difficult to complete troop quotas by relying solely on white volunteers. Soon, slaves were welcome in the ranks. New Hampshire offered bounties to any slaveholder who manumitted black recruits. Massachusetts authorized the recruitment of blacks in regular troop levies. Those who fought in the colonial army automatically received manumission, which was a term used for when a slave was freed.[91]

Despite these recruitment efforts, no one

considered abolishing slavery. Some American leaders feared abolition might disturb the unity of states, particularly in the South, and weaken the war effort. Thus, it was not surprising that the Massachusetts House of Representatives refused to pass legislation against slavery because of "apprehension that our brethren in other colonies should conceive there was an impropriety." [92]

All told, more than 4,000 blacks fought alongside the white colonists in the Revolutionary War. Nonetheless, not every colonial general was pleased to have black soldiers in his units.

"Is it consistent with the Sons of Liberty," General Philip Schuyler asked during the Saratoga campaign, "to trust their all to be defended by slaves?" General William Heath would only concede that his Negro troops "were generally able-bodied." Nevertheless, he said, he "was never pleased to see them mixing with white men." [93]

General Horatio Gates was an American who felt differently. He had only gratitude and praise for slaves "permitted to assist us in securing our freedom at the risk of their own lives." [94]

Although some blacks served in local militia units, most were to be found in the line regiments which bore the brunt of the fighting — in other words, the places where the most dangerous battles were fought. During the Rhode Island campaign of 1778, Colonel Christopher Greene's Negro regiment repulsed waves of Hessian troops in one of the bloodiest local actions of the war.[95] (Britain hired Hessians, who were German, to help with much of the fighting.) When the American army retreated at Brandywine in 1777 (a battle in which the Marquis de Lafayette himself was wounded), a Negro soldier in the Third Pennsylvania Artillery fought off the enemy with abandoned weapons until he could bring his ammunition wagon to safety.[96]

If anyone appreciated the efforts of Negro soldiers, then surely the enemy did. A Hessian officer serving with General Burgoyne noted that no American regiment "is to be seen in which there are not Negroes in abundance; and among them are able-bodied and strong and brave fellows."[97]

Black soldiers were there when a British offensive failed in the fall of 1777. British and Hessian soldiers had gone on the offensive at a place called Freeman's Farm (no relation to Bett) On Oct. 17, ten days after the action began, this

British regiment surrendered near the village of Saratoga. Certainly the British and Germans were not happy to be prisoners of war. Still, some of them would later write of their shock when they came face to face with American troops. These "troops" were composed of "oddly clothed young boys and old men in the militia ranks, and Negroes who presented arms as free men along with free men." Some of these POWs would write how they thought they were seeing a new race of men ... a race that included blacks.[98]

But it's important to remember that not every black fought on the American side. Some 3,000 black soldiers joined the British regiments. The British kept their promise and gave the former slaves a haven after the war. Some ex-slaves were known to have settled as far away as Eastern Europe.[99]

The war must have been a difficult but exhilarating time for all soldiers, black or white. In a letter dated Feb. 19, 1777, to Theodore Sedgwick, his close friend Erastus Sergeant writes, "my situation is new and tho' (sic) the habitation of war, the din of drums and the clashing of arms

... yet I must truly say there is a great beauty in a well-disciplined army, there is such a rotation of harmony from the general to the sentinel, that a mind disposed to order will most readily acquiesce."[100]

Not everyone agreed with Sergeant. A letter in the Theodore Sedgwick collection at the Massachusetts Historical Society in Boston, (Sedgwick's grandson, Theodore III, found the letter in 1831), signed by no other than Samuel Chase and Charles Carroll of Carrollton, includes the following: "we are sorry to find so little discipline in the army, and that it is so badly provided in every respect. We have some time since written pressingly to Congress for hard money, without which we believe it impossible to relieve our wants."[101]

It must have been difficult to demand discipline and order from an army that was suffering so much. An account of Benedict Arnold's 1775 march to Quebec revealed just how hard life in the colonial army could be. In the march, American troops took twice as much time as expected and quickly used up half of their provisions. Things then went from bad to worse: boats carrying provisions were overturned in rapids and accidentally destroyed during long hauls up waterfalls. Constant rain destroyed much of what was left of their food. Soon Arnold's men were boiling and eating rawhide. On Oct. 15, while camping at Dead River, Colonel Christopher Greene's men boiled their candles into a gruel. The commander of the Connecticut division, Roger Enos, decided to turn back. His retreat actually ended up helping the expedition. There would be more food — such as it was — left for the remaining soldiers.[102]

As commander-in-chief, George Washington spent an inordinate amont of his time worrying about his troops' health. Illness was rampant in the camps and clothes and food were in short supply. Finally, Washington finally wrote to Congress: "The Cry of want of Provisions comes to me from every Quarter ... Consider, I beseech you, the consequences of this neglect and exert yourself to remedy this evil."[103]

In light of all this, Theodore Sedgwick's wartime job was an important one. For a time, he was in charge of obtaining food and supplies, such as cattle, for the army.[104] Whatever doubts his friend John Ashley may have had about the cause, he'd long ago put them aside. He was generous with his money, time and influence during the Revolutionary War.

Chapter 6

Catharine Sedgwick described her friend Elizabeth Freeman as having a character "composed of few and strong elements."

Action was the law of her nature — conscious of superiority to all around her a state of servitude was intolerable. It was not the work, work was play to her. Her power of executive was marvellous. Nor was it awe of her kind master or fear of her despotic mistress. But it was the gulling of the harness, the irrepressible longing for liberty.[105]

Bett must have also been a high profile person in her community, and not just because she belonged to John Ashley. According to 1776 Massachusetts census figures only 216 blacks lived in the Berkshires. (The largest black population that year was in Essex County, with 1,049 blacks.)[106] If Bett was indeed as intelligent as

Catharine says she was, local abolitionists may have asked her to file a test case against her master.

Another of John Ashley's slaves, Zach Mullen, had filed a similar suit against him, prior to Bett's. Mullen's case was repeatedly postponed, which may mean that Bett's suit was indeed considered the freedom test case of the Berkshires.[107] Catharine Sedgwick's account of Bett's decision says nothing about test cases of any sort. (One can only assume, though, that Bett paid close attention to Zach Mullen's doings.) According to Catharine's story, Bett attended a gathering at the Sheffield meeting house (the one her master had helped build years earlier) whereupon the Declaration of Independence was read. Bett listened along with everyone else, then went to the office of attorney Theodore Sedgwick the next day.

Catharine's description of their meeting is stirring.

"Sir," Bett said, "I heard that paper read yesterday that all men are born equal and that every man has a right to freedom. I am not a dumb critter. Won't the law give me my freedom?"[108]

Catharine writes, "I can imagine her upright form as she stood ... with her fresh hope based on the declaration of her intrinsic inalienable right. Such a resolve as hers is like God's messenger; wind, snow and hail, irresistible." [109]

Another account of the conversation between Bett and Sedgwick is provided by yet another woman novelist, Harriet Martineau. Martineau, a woman with strong abolitionist leanings, visited the Berkshires a few years after Bett's death, and became a friend of the Sedgwick family.

According to Martineau's account, Sedgwick asked Bett how she had learned "the doctrine and facts on which she proceeded.", She replied, "By keepin' still and mindin' things.'" Martineau says Sedgwick then asked Bett what sort of things she'd minded. Bett is said to have described "for instance, when she was waiting at table, she heard gentlemen talking over the Bill of Rights and the new constitution of Massachusetts; and in all they said she never heard but that all people were born free and equal and she thought long about it, and resolved she would try whether she did not come in among them." [110]

Henry Sedgwick gave yet another version: it was the heated shovel incident which sent Bett to

Sedgwick's office. Catharine's essay, though, definitely puts Bett's injury in another category. It was not Hannah Ashley's cruelty but American ideals of freedom that prompted Bett to file her lawsuit, Catharine wrote.

Why did Bett choose Sedgwick? In Catharine's obviously prejudiced opinion, Bett's request was made to "one who had the generosity as well as the intelligence to meet it."[111] One can also safely assume that Bett was a savvy woman who understood the politics and the ins and outs of her community. Theodore Sedgwick may have been young (35 at the time), but he was also a rising star. He was considered the leading attorney in Sheffield. He would one day serve as Speaker of the House of Representatives and as a justice on the Massachusetts Supreme Court. Sedgwick, a Yale graduate (also Ashley's alma mater), also had Connecticut attorney Tapping Reeve for a mentor. Reeve, of Litchfield, founder of the Litchfield Law School, was considered one of the best legal minds of his day.

Bett might also have sensed a kindness in Sedgwick. He was a devoted family man who would eventually father 10 children. His wife, Pamela Dwight Sedgwick, often suffered from poor health. Sedgwick's career frequently kept him away from home but he did his best to check on her while he was gone.

However, Sedgwick was also a friend of John Ashley. As noted earlier, they'd worked together on Berkshire declarations of independence. He must have visited with Ashley on social occasions; more than likely this was how he met Bett.

So, why did Sedgwick say yes? No one really knows. Sedgwick is said to have been reluctant to take on Bett's case — understandable, considering the circumstances. He had not yet become a well-respected congressman or jurist. John Ashley was a friend, colleague and neighbor. Sedgwick had undoubtedly enjoyed Ashley's hospitality on many occasions.

Still, Bett's request stirred something in Sedgwick, and he took the case. He is described in a Boston Bar Journal article as having been intrigued by the "palpable illogic of slavery at a time when Massachusetts was engaged in a fight for freedom from imperial regulation and control."[112] Some historians suggest that he did so because he (and others) wanted to mount a constitutional challenge to slavery. Later on in his life Sedgwick did join an abolitionist (anti-slavery) society. On the other hand, long before he took on Bett's case he did own slaves. In the end, the only thing we can assume about Sedgwick is that he thought Bett's case was winnable.

He was up against some top legal talent. Ashley was represented in court by David Noble, who later served as a judge of the Court of Common Pleas and a trustee of Williams College, and John Canfield, a prominent attorney from Sharon, Conn. On the other hand, Sedgwick had Reeve on his side; the Connecticut lawyer assisted his protege throughout the case.[113] Reeve and Sedgwick soon had two petitioners to worry about. Somewhere along the line Bett was joined in her suit by another one of Ashley's slaves, a man named Brom. We know nothing about Brom except that the Ashleys owned him and like Bett, he wanted to be free. (There has never been any indication as to why Lizzie did not join her sister in the freedom suit.)

The suit began with a writ of replevin, filed by Sedgwick in the Berkshire County Court of Common Pleas on May 28, 1781. This writ, an action for a recovery of property, was instituted on the grounds that Bett and Brom were not the legitimate property of the Ashleys. Two writs were sent to Ashley and also to his son, John III, an army general who'd play a crucial role in quelling the insurgents of Shays Rebellion. (Writer Jon Swan suggests in his *American Heritage* article that the elusive Brom may have actually lived in the younger Ashley's household.)[114]

The writ demanded Ashley release the pair, but he refused. Brom and Bett were his servants for life, he said. He claimed " a right of servitude in the Persons of the said Brom and Bett." [115]

John Ashley may have been a kind and mild person, but he was not about to willingly let Bett and Brom go. The local authorities made several attempts to retrieve the slaves, only to be rebuffed by Ashley. Finally the court ordered their release. A court date for *Brom & Bett vs. J. Ashley Esq.* was set for Aug. 21, 1781.[116] Ashley's attorneys immediately asked for a dismissal and abatement on the grounds that "the said Brom and Bett are and were at the time of Issuing the original wit the legal Negro Servants of the said John Ashley during their lives, and this the said John Ashley is ready to verify and here of prays the Judgment of this Court and the suit may be abated." [117]

The account of what Sedgwick and his mentor

said to the jury in court is provided by the Duc de la Rochefoucauld-Liancourt. The Duc visited the United States between 1795 and 1797. At some point in his travels he visited Sedgwick in Stockbridge. In the account he wrote of that trip, *Travels*, the Duc discloses that Reeve and Sedgwick "argued that no antecedent law had established slavery, and that the laws that seemed to suppose it were the offspring of error in the legislators ... and that such laws even if they had existed, were annulled by the new constitution."[118]

The jury, headed by foreman Jonathan Holcomb, needed only a short time to decide that Brom and Bett were not, and had never been, the legal servants of Ashley. They awarded 30 shillings in damages and ordered Ashley to pay court costs. Ashley did appeal, but dropped it in the fall. He may have been discouraged by the ruling in *Walker vs. Jennison*, a freedom lawsuit filed in Barre, Massachusetts. The master in that case, Nathaniel Jennison, lost his appeal of an earlier trial decision that had freed his slave.

Some historians like Lillian Preis also wonder if Ashley was still smarting from his association with the " infamous 17." He may have withdrawn his appeal to avoid bad publicity.[119] Nevertheless,

Historian Arthur Zilversmit, in a talk delivered at a Berkshire County Historical Society meeting in 1969, noted that the legal talent alone in the case shows that the Elizabeth Freeman case was an important one. Zilversmit opined that along with other court cases, including Caldwell vs. Jennison, the Freeman case helped end slavery in Massachusetts.[120]

Chapter 7

No discussion of the Elizabeth Freeman lawsuit is complete without also looking at *Walker vs. Jennison*, or the Quok Walker case. Quok Walker is widely considered to be the man whose court case ended slavery in Massachusetts. Walker was a slave living in Barre when his original master died. His master's widow then married a man named Nathaniel Jennison. Walker insisted that his late master promised to free him when he turned 25.

"I was ... 10 years old when master Caldwell died," Walker would later testify in court. " Mrs. lived a number of years before she married again. ... My old master said I should be free at 24 or 25 ... Mistress told me I should be free at 21 ..." But Jennison refused to honor either promise.[121]

In the spring of 1781 (around the time Bett asked Sedgwick for help with her lawsuit) Walker decided he'd had enough. He walked away from the Jennison home and hired himself out to some neighbors, John and Seth Caldwell. Jennison discovered where he was working and went to the Caldwell home to fetch him. But Walker refused to go with Jennison. Jennison returned, this time with a group of friends. Walker was beaten and then locked up for several hours.[122] But Walker didn't give up. In June of that year, two months before Bett's court victory, he sued Jennison for assault and battery in the Worcester Court of Common Pleas and won. The court also ruled that Walker was not Jennison's slave and did not have to obey him. Jennison argued, unsuccessfully, that upon marriage to Walker's master's widow, the slave had become his property.[123] Jennison appealed the case and the matter ended up in the Massachusetts' Supreme Court.

The court's Chief Justice William Cushing wrote this stirring opinion as the case was decided:

(Slavery) is a usage which took its origin from the practice of European nations and the British

government. But ... a different idea has taken place, with the people of America favorable to the natural rights of man, to that natural, innate desire for liberty ... All men are born free and equal. Every subject is entitled to liberty and to have it guarded. This being the case I think the idea of slavery is inconsistent with our conduct and constitution and there can be no such thing as perpetual servitude of a rational creature.[124]

Cushing declares proudly in his notes that this was the case by which "slavery in Massachusetts was forever abolished."[125] But the case wasn't over yet. Sore loser that he was, Jennison asked the legislature to reinstate his appeal. Jennison wanted a legislative declaration reversing the courts or, failing that, compensation for the loss of his slave.

The House passed a compromise bill saying that there never were legal slaves in Massachusetts and providing indemnity for all masters who'd heretofore held slaves; however, the bill went no further.

Some historians have even argued that because the legislature never outlawed slavery it was actually legal — though not practiced — in Massachusetts until the federal government banned it after the Civil War.

However, because the Quok Walker decision was such a high profile case and garnered such an eloquent opinion from Justice Cushing, many historians still consider it to be the case that ended slavery in the Bay State. Walker even got a mention in H.G. Well's *Outline of History.* Wells lists in *History* what he considered *the* two important events between 1780 and 1787. One was the Treaty of Paris and the other was the Quok Walker decision. [126]

The death of slavery in Massachusetts, it should be noted, was on money as much as it was fairness. In his book, *Black Bondage in the North*, Edgar J. McManus pointed out that the rapid growth of a white workforce (in sharp contrast to that of the early days of the settlement when workers of any color were rare) also led to slavery's end. White job-seekers didn't want slaves to fill jobs they could have themselves. [127] It was a factor of abolition that even John Adams addressed. "The common people would not suffer the labour, by which alone they could obtain a subsistence, to be done by slaves," Adams said. "If the gentlemen had been permitted by law to hold slaves the common people would have put the Negroes to death, and their masters too, perhaps."[128]

Chapter 8

Bett spent the next stage of her life in the household of Theodore Sedgwick. (No one bothered to record what happened to Brom or Lizzie; both disappeared into history.) Immediately after the trial, Sedgwick hired her as a paid domestic servant and nanny to his children.

By the time she came to live with him, Sedgwick owned a clapboard Temple-style Greek Revival home, built in the 1760s, on what is now Route 7, the Main Street of Sheffield. The family would later move to an equally attractive home in Stockbridge. As a nanny, Bett left a powerful impression on the Sedgwick children.

"The children under her government regarded it as ... a sort of theocracy ... a divine right were founded upon such ability and fidelity as hers," Catharine wrote.[129]

The Sedgwicks apparently needed her steady hand. Pamela Dwight Sedgwick appears to have suffered from some sort of mental illness or depression. Since Theodore traveled a lot, he counted on close friends like Erastus Sergeant to check in on Pamela and the children. In a letter dated Nov. 20, 1791, Sergeant tells Sedgwick: "I make it my daily business to call on (Pamela) and spent the last evening with her. She was in some degree variable, and a smile on her countenance. She attends to her family matters but everything is a burden to her — she says she can give no reason for her feelings, appears to be anxious about herself — is very unwilling that you know anything about it as it will only distress you when it is out of your power to render her any comfort. Your friends have been silent with regards to her in hopes she would be better, (but) she has remained much the same for about four weeks."[130]

It seems that Bett got along better with Pamela Sedgwick than anyone else, with the possible exception of her husband. "Mumbet was the only person who could tranquilize my mother when her mind was disordered — the only one of her friends she looked to have about her — and why?" Catharine Sedgwick wrote in her essay. She treated her with the same respect she did when she was sane. As far as possible she obeyed her commands and humored her caprices; in short, her superior instincts hit upon a mode of treatment that science had since adopted." [131] As if their family troubles weren't enough, the Sedgwicks were living in turbulent times. In 1786 and 1787 Shays' Rebellion would cause havoc in Massachusetts. This uprising was an aftershock of the American Revolution caused by the excessive land taxation, high legal costs, and the economic depression that followed the war.

Shay's Rebellion was one of many protests that took place after the war. The Shay's "rebels" were mostly poor farmers threatened with losing their property and being imprisoned because of their debts. The rebel's leader, Daniel Shay, had been a captain in the American Revolution army. He and his followers demanded that the Court of Common Pleas (where Bett and Brom had won their freedom), be abolished and that taxes be reduced.

In 1786, armed mobs prevented the sitting of the courts in North Hampton, Worcester, Great

Barrington, and Concord. Shay and his men broke up a session of the state Supreme Court in Springfield. On January 25, 1787, Shay marched into Springfield to seize the federal arsenal. They were repulsed by a force of militia under General Benjamin Lincoln. The rebels then fled toward Petersham, where they were finally defeated. Most of the rebels eventually received a pardon. Shay was condemned to death, but escaped to Vermont where he, too, received a pardon a year later. In the end, Shay's Rebellion and the other protests did their job: they forced the American leaders and politicians to pay attention to some serious problems, namely that the existing Articles of Confederation, which heretofore had provided the basic laws of the country, were not a good way to run things. Shay's Rebellion helped push the nation's leaders closer to formulating and ratifying the constitution of the young United States.

Of course, all of this was little comfort to the Sedgwicks, like other wealthy Stockbridge families, who lived in fear of looters. On a day while Theodore was away, it was up to Bett to defend the family home against a band of rebels.

She used what we might call a "feminine" form

of defense. She shooed Pamela Sedgwick and the children into hiding and faced the intruders alone. She apparently intimidated them with the sheer force of her personality, diversionary tactics and a heavy dose of sarcasm. For example, the leader of the group that had invaded the Sedgwick home took a fancy to Theodore's favorite horse, Jenny Gray. His possession of the horse proved short-lived, thanks to Jenny Gray and Bett. The mare threw him as soon as he climbed aboard.

While the man was still on the ground, recovering from his fall, Bett shooed the mare to the pasture and out of the rebel's grasp.[132] The men then demanded access to the Sedgwicks' stock of top-quality liquors. Bett brought them a keg of common brown stout (beer) instead. The stout became enough of a diversion that the rebels forgot about the higher-quality stock they'd asked for.[133] Bett had already hidden the family valuables in a chest that contained her own things. (According to Catharine Sedgwick, Bett had some fine baubles of her own. "Mum Bett had a regal love of the solid and splendid wear and the last of her long life went on accumulating chintzes and silks," Catharine wrote.)[134] The rebels spied the chest and demanded that she open it. Bett turned the tables and dared them to open it themselves.

"You call me wench and nigger," she told them. "And you are not above rummaging my chest. You will have to break it open to do it." Bett's defiance was apparently too much for them. The rebels backed off, let the chest alone and went on their way.[135] Shay's Rebellion appears to be the last dramatic episode in Bett's long life. She kept working in the Sedgwick house, saved her money and bought a little house of her own nearby. She went on collecting the silks and chintzes she enjoyed. As she aged, Bett became a beloved "elder stateswoman" in her community.

Bett's biological family also gathered around her as she aged. She seems to have seen a lot of her daughter, grandchildren and great-grandchildren, though Catharine Sedgwick appeared to feel Bett's family depended on her far too much.[136]

When Bett was in her 60s, Susan Sedgwick, Theodore's daughter-in-law and the wife of his eldest son Theodore Jr., painted her portrait, the only known likeness of Elizabeth Freeman. Bett sat for the portrait in a pale, robin's egg-blue dress, ivory-colored head scarf and a favorite necklace of gold beads. Susan took liberties with her subject in that she put the scar from the infamous heated shovel incident on Bett's forehead instead of her arm.[137] The portrait is a watercolor on ivory, 4½ by 3¾ inches. It was donated to the Massachusetts Historical Society on Valentine's Day, 1884, by Susan's daughter Maria. (The gold-bead necklace was later made into a bracelet. It is also in the permanent collection of the Massachusetts Historical Society.)

Susan herself followed in Catharine's footsteps to became a novelist of some note. Born Susan Anne Livingston Ridley, granddaughter of Governor William Livingston of New Jersey, she'd married Theodore Jr. in 1808. Susan spent much of her time at the family home in Stockbridge (and must have gotten to know Bett well) while her husband practiced law in Albany, New York. After Theodore Jr. retired from the law in 1821, Susan took up writing. She wrote "moralistic" children's novels whereupon children and women had heroic qualities that allow them to overcome unfortunate, and often improbable, circumstances. [138]

Chapter 9

An intriguing postscript to Bett's life is the story that she may have married again, later in life and quite auspiciously. This second marriage would put her in the family line of one of Black America's great social activists.

A biographer of W.E.B. DuBois, considered by many to be the father of the Civil Rights movement, mentions an ancestor of DuBois named Elizabeth Freeman Burghhardt, also known as Mum Bett.[139] William Edward Burghardt DuBois was born in Great Barrington in 1868, more than 30 years after Bett died. DuBois grew up on the farm of his maternal grandfather, Othello. He went on to become the first black to receive a doctoral degree from

Harvard University. (His doctoral thesis covered the theme, *The Suppression of the African Slave Trade in the United States of America.*) Before he turned thirty, he had completed the first sociological study of blacks in the United States, in a work entitled, *The Philadelphia Negro*. In 1910, DuBois arranged to bring an organization he led, the Niagara Movement, into the newly-formed National Association for the Advancement of Colored People. (NAACP). [140]

DuBois wrote that Othello Burghardt had been a stepson of Elizabeth Freeman Burghardt. The family, known as the Black Burghardts, were well-known in the area. (Bett is said to have married Jack Burghardt, Othello's father. This would make her DuBois' step-great-grandmother.)[141] The Sedgwicks, however, never mentioned a remarriage. In fact, they talk of Bett as though she remained a widow throughout her life. Moreover, she was buried in the Sedgwick family plot. Yet, DuBois does have his story and it's a tempting one.

Bett died in 1829, leaving behind an estate of about $1,000. Her will, drawn up by one of

Theodore's sons, bequeaths her home to her daughter Elizabeth. It also bequeaths individual items, clothes and jewelry, to her grandchildren and great-grandchildren.[142]

Bett was buried alongside the the Sedgwick family in Stockbridge. Her grave rests near the center of the family circle, beside Catharine's. Theodore's son Charles wrote this epitaph for her:

> She was born a slave and remained a slave for nearly 30 years. She could neither read nor write, yet in her own sphere she had no superior or equal. She neither wasted time nor property. She never violated a trust, nor failed to perform a duty. In every situation of domestic trial, she was the most efficient helper and the tenderest friend. Good Mother, farewell.[143]

Bett had used her freedom well. She had built a comfortable life for herself. But many other blacks were years, even generations, away from enjoying such a life. The U.S. Constitution, when ratified, had not abolished slavery. At the time Bett died, the Civil War was more than 30 years in the future and the Civil Rights movement was a century away. In Massachusetts, blacks may not have been slaves but they *were* second-class citizens.

There were northern masters who rushed to cash in on their slave holdings. Some sent pregnant women out of state so that their children could not claim freedom under new abolition statutes. Some slavers went as far as seizing blacks on the streets and exporting them south. Exporting blacks to the South or West Indies was illegal but masters would attempt it anyway. Other masters simply got around the law by signing their slaves to incredibly long indentures. They'd then sell them as slaves to masters in slave-owning states. Census figures show that in the 18th and 19th centuries the black population declined in almost every Northern state. Those who stayed put did not feel welcome. Interracial marriages was still outlawed and blacks were discouraged from settling in a new home. Massachusetts prescribed flogging for nonresident blacks who remained for longer than two months. They also couldn't vote in elections.[144] White workers had protested for years that competition from slaves was unfair but as long as slaveholders turned a profit from the system, nothing was done about it. When slavery ended, blacks had to enter the labor market without protection and were pushed out of one line of work after another. The whites who'd once felt that slavery pushed wages down or kept unemployment levels high would not tolerate black competitors. The more immigrants that entered the country, the larger the white work force grew. Whites wanted to protect their jobs at the expense of former slaves.

It was left to Frederick Douglass to observe: "Every hour sees the black man elbowed out of employment by some newly arrived immigrant whose hunger and whose color are thought to give him better title."[145]

Blacks who sought employment in Boston were insulted, threatened and even attacked. One observer even made this very sad comment: many Negroes would probably have been better off in their former state of slavery.[146]

Still, there were bright spots and signs of resiliency. Boston already had the makings of a strong black community by the time the revolutionary War ended. This community was in the city's West End, between Pinckney and

Cambridge Streets, and in a neighborhood which is now known as the North Slope of Beacon Hill, between Joy and Charles Street.

In 1787, six years after Bett's suit, Boston's Prince Hall was busier than ever trying to make life easier for his people. He lost a fight that year which would have forced the public school system to allow black students. Eleven years later, parents asked the city to set up separate schools for black children. This, too, was denied. Parents then set up a community school in Prince Hall's home, located at the northeast corner West Cedar and Revere Streets on Beacon Hill. In 1808, The Abiel Smith school was moved from the Hall home to the African Meeting House at 8 Smith Street. Built in 1805, the African Meeting House was, and is, the oldest black church in America. Before its construction, blacks had been worshipping in Faneuil Hall, at services led by the black preacher Thomas Paul. [147]

Beacon Hill eventually became the home of such prominent black Bostonians as John P. Coburn, who in 1851 was tried and acquitted for rescuing a fugitive slave, and the abolitionist Lewis Harden.[148]

Harden and his wife, Harriet, had escaped to

Boston in 1849 via the Underground Railroad. They subsequently turned their Phillips Street home into an Underground Railroad Station and befriended abolitionist author Harriet Beecher Stowe, who wrote *Uncle Tom's Cabin.* Harden went on to serve in the Massachusetts State Legislature. His estate was eventually used to set up a fund for black students who wanted to attend Harvard Medical School.[149]

This portion of Beacon Hill which so nurtured Boston's black community is now operated by the National Park Service as the Boston African American National Historic Site and the Black Heritage trail.

Afterword

Those of us with modern sensibilities would probably be happier if Bett had become a freedom fighter. We'd much prefer to imagine her giving speeches, leading marches or working in the Underground Railroad than to envision her washing clothes and minding yet another family's children. Yet, the events in Bett's life tell us that she was indeed a pragmatic woman. For her, living with and working for the Sedgwicks was a pragmatic decision and probably a necessary one. Women of Bett's era did not have the kind of choices women today have.

And yet, history is filled with examples of ordinary people doing extraordinary things. Almost two centuries after Bett filed her freedom suit, an unassuming woman named Rosa Parks changed history one hot summer's day by refusing to give up her seat on a bus. Park's simple act of defiance helped fuel the Civil Rights movement.

Like Rosa Parks, Elizabeth Freeman was an ordinary person who performed an remarkable act. Once her court was completed and she was free, Freeman went back to her ordinary life. She raised her daughter, saved her money, enjoyed her friends and neighbors, bought a home for herself and enjoyed collecting jewelry and fine clothing.

Yet, like Parks and the other ordinary people who came before and after her, Elizabeth Freeman helped to change the course of history. She is a reminder to all of us that one need not be famous, or a great speaker, or a great intellect to make a difference in the world. All one really needs to do is take a stand and stay the course, as Elizabeth Freeman did.

Bibliography

Black Heritage Trail. brochure. (researched by Byron Rushing, edited by staff of the Museum of Afro-American History) Boston African American National Historic Site, National Park Service.

Brom & Bett vs. J. Ashley Esq. Berkshire County Court of Common Pleas, 1781, Berkshire Atheneum.

Chronicles of Old Canaan, courtesy of the Sheffield Historical Society, Page 22.

Bulkeley, Morgan. "I, John Ashley of Sheffield," *Berkshire Courier*, June 4, 1970.

Cushing Family (William J.), *Personal Papers*, Massachusetts Historical Society, Boston, Mass.

Earle, Alice Morse. *Home Life in Colonial Days*. New York: The MacMillan Co., 1898.

Eckert, Allen W. *The Frontiersmen*. New York: Little, Brown & Co., 1967.

Felton, Harold W. *Mumbet: The Story of Elizabeth Freeman*. New York: Dodd, Mead and Albright, 1970.

Mumbet:

Haynes, Lindsay, Article in *The New York Times*, September 13, 1970.

MacDonald, Mimi. "Mum Bet's Freedom Struggle," The Berkshire Courier, July, 1981.

Meade, Homer. "W.E.B. DuBois, Father of the Modern Civil Rights Movement," *Berkshire Courier*, July, 1981.

McManus, Edgar J. *Black Bondage in the North*. Syracuse, New York: Syracuse University Press, 1973.

O'Brien, William S.J. "Slavery and the Jennison Case." *William & Mary Quarterly*. Volume XVIII. April, 1960.

Preiss, Lillian. *Sheffield, Frontier Town*. North Adams, Mass: Excelsior Printing Company, 1976.

Sedgwick, Catharine Maria. *Personal Papers*. Massachusetts Historical Society, Boston, Mass.

Sedgwick, Theodore. *Personal Papers*. Massachusetts Historical Society, Boston, Mass.

Swan, Jon. "The Slave Who Sued for Freedom," *American Heritage*. March, 1990. Pages 51-55.

The American Heritage Book of The Revolution (edited by Richard M. Ketchum). New York: American Heritage Publishing, 1957.

The Last Will and Testament of Elizabeth Freeman, Sheffield Family History Center, Sheffield, Massachusetts.

"The Single Known Portrait by A Singular Lady," (edited by Karen M. Jones). *Antiques*. date unknown.

Trowbridge, Francis Bacon. *The Ashley Genealogy*. New Haven: Press of Tuttle, Morehouse and Taylor, 1896.

Twombly, Robert. "Black Resistance to Slavery in Massachusetts." *Insights and Parallels: Problems and issues of American Social History* (Edited by William O'Neill). Minneapolis: Burgess Publishing, 1973.

Zilversmit, Arthur. "Mumbet: Folklore and Fact." Taken from a speech given to the Berkshire Historical Society. 1969. Sheffield Family History Center, Sheffield Massachusetts.

Zilversmit, Arthur. "Quok Walker, Mumbet and the Abolition of Slavery in Massachusetts." *William & Mary Quarterly*. Volume XXV (1968).

Endnotes

1 Catharine Maria Sedgwick, essay on Mumbet, undated, Catharine Maria Sedgwick Papers, Massachusetts Historical Society, Boston, Mass.

2 The Last Will and Testament of Elizabeth Freeman, Family History Center, Sheffield, Mass.

3 Haynes, Lindsay, *The New York Times*, September 13, 1970.

4 Ibid.

5 Ibid.

6 Preiss, Lillian. *Sheffield, Frontier Town*, Excelsior Printing Company, (North Adams, Mass-achusetts: 1976). page 108.

7 Bulkeley, Morgan. I, "John Ashley of Sheffield," *Berkshire Courier*, June 4, 1970.

8 *Chronicles of Old Canaan*, Page 22.

9 MacDonald, Mimi. "Mum Bet's Freedom Struggle," *Berkshire Courier*, July, 1981, Page 3.

10 Felton, Harold W. *Mumbet, the Story of Elizabeth Freeman*. New York: Dodd, Mead and Alright, 1970, Page 16.

11 Ibid., Page 1.

12 Catherine Maria Sedgwick, essay on Mumbet, undated, Catharine Maria Sedgwick Papers.

13 MacDonald, Page 1.

14 Freeman will.

15 Felton, Page 9.

16 MacDonald, Page 3.

17 *Black Heritage Trail*, brochure. (researched by Byron Rushing, edited by staff of the Museum of Afro-American History), Boston African American National Historic Site, National Park Service.

18 McManus, Edgar J. *Black Bondage in the North*. Syracuse: Syracuse University Press, 1973, Page 19.

Mumbet:

19 Catharine Maria Sedgwick, essay on Mumbet.

20 Swan, Jon. "The Slave Who Sued for Freedom," *American Heritage*, March, 1990, Page 52.

21 Twombly, Robert C. Black Resistance to Slavery." *Insights and Parallels: Problems and Issues of American Social History* (Edited by William O'Neill). Minneapolis: Burgess Publishing, 1973.

22 McManus, Page 21-22.

23 Ibid., Page 7.

24 Ibid.,Page 17.

25 Ibid.,Page 42.

26 Ibid.

27 Ibid., Page 43.

28 Ibid., Page 45.

29 Ibid., Page 96.

30 Earle, Alice. *Homelife in Colonial Days*. New York: The MacMillan Co., 1898.

31 Twombly, Page 26.

32 Ibid.

33 Ibid.

34 Ibid., Page 27.

35 Ibid., Page 28.

36 Ibid.

37 McManus, Page 92.

38 Ibid., Page 93.

39 Ibid., Page 29.

40 Ibid.

41 Ibid., Page 30.

42 Ibid.

43 McManus, Page 90.

44 Ibid., Page 46.

45 Ibid., Page 81.

46 Ibid., Page 108.

47 Twombly, Page 23.

48 Ibid.

49 Ibid., Page 24.

50 Ibid.

51 Ibid., Page 25.

52 Ibid.

53 Ibid., Page 14.

54 Ibid.

55 Ibid.

56 Ibid., Page 17.

57 McManus, Page 63-64.

58 Ibid., Page 65.

59 Ibid., Page 66.

60 Ibid., Page 67.

61 Haynes .

62 Ibid.

63 Twombly, Page 14.

64 Catharine Maria Sedgwick, essay on Mumbet, undated, Catharine Maria Sedgwick Papers.

65 Preiss, Page 77.

66 Ibid., Page 110.

67 Ibid., Page 35.

68 Trowbridge, Francis Bacon. *The Ashley Genealogy*. New Haven: Press of Tuttle, Morehouse and Taylor, 1896, Page 56.

69 Preiss, Page 35.

70 Catharine Maria Sedgwick, essay on Mumbet, undated, Catharine Maria Sedgwick Papers.

71 Ibid.

72 Ibid.

73 Zilversmit, " Mumbet: Folklore and Fact," Page 5.

74 Catharine Maria Sedgwick, essay on Mumbet, undated, Catharine Maria Sedgwick Papers.

75 Eckert, Allen W. *The Frontiersmen*. New York: Little, Brown & Co., 1967.

76 Preiss, Page 37.

77 Ibid.

78 Ibid., Page 37-38.

79 Ibid., Page 38.

80 Ibid.

81 Ibid., Page 44.

82 Ibid.

83 Ibid., Page 40.

84 Ibid.

85 Ibid., Page 42.

87 Ibid.

88 Ibid., Page 43.

89 Ibid., Page 42.

90 McManus, Page 154.

91 Ibid., Page 155.

92 Ibid., Page 161.

93 Ibid., Page 156.

94 Ibid., Page 156-157.

95 Ibid., Page 157.

96 Ibid.

97 McManus, Pages 158-159.

98 *The American Heritage Book of The Revolution* (edited by Richard M. Ketchum). New York: American Heritage Publishing, 1957, Pages 247-248 .

99 McManus, Page 159.

100 Erastus Sergeant to Theodore Sedgwick, 19 Feb. 1777, Theodore Sedgwick I Papers, Massachusetts Historical Society.

101 Samuel Chase and Charles Carroll to [ ], 26 May 1776, Theodore Sedgwick I Papers.

102 Heritage, Pages 123-124.

103 Ibid., Page 210.

104 An account of cattle purchased and forwarded to [Elisha] Avery, 1775, Theodore Sedgwick I Papers.

105 Catharine Sedgwick, essay on Mumbet, undated, Catharine Maria Sedgwick Papers.

106 McManus, Page 199.

107 Zilversmit, "Mumbet: Folklore and Fact," Page 11.

108 Catharine Sedgwick, essay on Mumbet, undated, Catharine Maria Sedgwick Papers.

109 Ibid.

110 Swan, Page 54.

111 Catharine Maria Sedgwick, essay on Mumbet, undated, Catharine Maria Sedgwick Papers.

112 Preiss, Lilian, Page 48.

113 Swan, Page 54.

114 Ibid.

115 Zilversmit, "Quok Walker, Mumbet and the Abolition of Slavery in Massachusetts."

116 Ibid.

117 Ibid.

118 Swan, Page 54.

119 Preiss, Page 48.

120 Zilversmit, "Mumbet: Fact and Folklore," Page 12.

121 William Cushing, judicial notebook on the Quok Walker case, 1783, Cushing Family Papers.

122 O'Brien, William S.J. "Did the Jennison Case End Slavery in Massachusetts." *William & Mary Quarterly*. Volume XVIII. April, 1960.

123 Ibid.

124 William Cushing, judicial notebook on the Quok Walker case, 1783, Cushing Family Papers.

125 Ibid.

126 O'Brien, William.

127 McManus, Page 180.

128 Ibid., Page 166.

129 Catharine Maria Sedgwick, essay on Mumbet, undated, Catharine Maria Sedgwick Papers.

130 Erastus Sergeant to Theodore Sedgwick, 20 Nov. 1791, Theodore Sedgwick I Papers.

Mumbet:

131 Catharine Maria Sedgwick, essay on Mumbet, undated, Catharine Maria Sedgwick Papers.

132 Ibid.

133 Ibid.

134 Ibid.

135 Ibid.

136 Ibid.

137 "The Single Known Portrait by A Singular Lady" (edited by Karen M. Jones), *Antiques*. date unknown.

138 Ibid.

139 Meade, Homer. "W.E.B. DuBois, Father of the Modern Civil Rights Movement," *Berkshire Courier*, July, 1981.

140 Ibid.

141 Ibid.

142 Freeman Will.

143 Preis, Page 49.

144 McManus, Page 182.

145 Ibid., Page 184.

146 Ibid., Page 185.

147 Black Heritage Trail.

148 Ibid.

149 Ibid.

Index